John Rodgers

The faithful Servant rewarded

A Sermon delivered at Princeton, before the Board of Trustees of the

College of New-Jersey

John Rodgers

The faithful Servant rewarded
A Sermon delivered at Princeton, before the Board of Trustees of the College of New-Jersey

ISBN/EAN: 9783337172718

Printed in Europe, USA, Canada, Australia, Japan

Cover: Foto ©ninafisch / pixelio.de

More available books at **www.hansebooks.com**

THE

FAITHFUL SERVANT REWARDED:

A

S E R M O N,

DELIVERED AT PRINCETON,

BEFORE THE BOARD OF TRUSTEES OF THE COLLEGE OF
NEW-JERSEY, MAY 6, 1795, OCCASIONED BY THE DEATH OF

The Rev. JOHN WITHERSPOON, D. D. L. L. D.

PRESIDENT OF SAID COLLEGE.

———————

BY JOHN RODGERS, D. D.

SENIOR MINISTER OF THE UNITED PRESBYTERIAN
CHURCHES, IN THE CITY OF NEW-YORK.

══════════════════

NEW-YORK—PRINTED BY THOMAS GREENLEAF.
1795.

ADVERTISEMENT.

THE *following discourse was prepared at the pressing request of a number of the trustees of the college, to be delivered at the first meeting of the board after the late president's death. This meeting was unavoidably delayed until the fifth instant; as the trustees wished to fill the vacant chair, the first time they met —but this could not be done, by an ordinance of the board, of an early date, until after a certain period from the time of the commencement of the vacancy.*

The board being met, they passed the following resolves :

May 5th. **On** *motion resolved unanimously, that the reverend Dr. Rodgers be requested to preach a funeral sermon on the death of the reverend Dr. Witherspoon, late president of the college, to-morrow, at 11 o'clock A. M. in the church.*

May 6th. **The** *board attended upon the delivery of the sermon on the death of the late president, and having met—On motion resolved unanimously, that the thanks of the board be given to Dr. Rodgers for his sermon; and that Dr. Boudinot, Mr. Roe and Col. Bayard, be a committee to request a copy for publication.*

WALTER MINTO,
Clerk of the Board.

New-York, May 15th, 1795.

FAITHFUL SERVANT REWARDED.

MATTHEW xxv. 21.

" *His Lord faid unto him, Well done thou good and faithful Servant ; thou haft been faithful over a few things, I will make thee ruler over many things ; enter thou into the joy of thy Lord.*"

THE doctrine of a future ftate of rewards and punifhments, lies deep at the foundation of our holy religion : It is a doctrine perfectly confonant to reafon, and fupported by it; and is either afferted, or juftly taken for granted, in every page of the facred oracles. This is the immortality, for the bleffednefs of which we became incapacitated, by our apoftacy from God ; and that, for the enjoyment of which, it is one great defign of the religion of Jefus Chrift to prepare us. The whole frame of this religion is wifely calculated for this end. Among the many evidences of thefe truths, we may appeal to the difcourfes of our Divine Mafter; and particularly to this, of which our text is a part.

In the preceding chapter, he had given his difciples an inftructive difcourfe on the certainty and folemnity of his fecond coming. He continues the fubject in this chapter, and enforces the great duty

of preparation for it, by the parable of the ten vir-
gins, from the firſt verſe to the thirteenth ; by the
parable of the talents, from thence to the thirtieth
verſe ; and by a more particular account of the
proceſs of the judgment of the great day, from
thence to the end of the chapter.

The more immediate deſign of the parable of the
talents, of which our text is a part, is to enforce
the duty, and illuſtrate the happineſs of being prepared for *giving up our account,* when he ſhall come
to judge the world in righteouſneſs. You may
read it at your leiſure. The " man travelling into a far country," in this parable, means our Lord
himſelf ; who is the great head of his church,
which is his family. The "ſervants," of whom
we here read, mean all profeſſing Chriſtians ; all
who call themſelves the ſervants of Chriſt, whatever their nation or denomination may be ; though
ſome ſuppoſe, theMiniſters of the Goſpel are more
particularly intended.

By the *talents,* we are to underſtand the various
gifts of Heaven, whether of a common or of a
ſpecial nature. They include the bounties of Providence, ſuch as health, ſtrength, reaſon, riches,
honour, power, learning, reputation, the ſeveral
advantages ariſing from our ſtations in life ; and,
together with theſe, thoſe graces of the ſpirit that
conſtitute the Chriſtian temper. Theſe are all
ſo many talents put into our hands, to be improved
for God, and the beſt intereſts of our fellow-crea-
tures ; and they are different to different perſons.
To one God gives more of theſe gifts or graces,
and to another leſs ; which is deſigned in the parable by the maſter's giving to one ſervant *five* talents, and to another *two,* and to another *one.*

By " the Lord of thofe fervants coming, after a long time, to reckon with them," we are to underſtand that particular judgment which every one paſſes under at death, when their final ſtates are determined : and alſo, and principally, our Lord's coming to judge the world in righteouſneſs, at the laſt day, " When every one ſhall receive the things done in the body, according to that he hath done, whether it be good or bad." At both theſe ſolemn periods, the faithful fervant of Chriſt, whatever his character and ſtation in life may have been, ſhall be received with a " Well done, thou good and faithful fervant ; thou haſt been faithful over a few things, I will make thee ruler over many things ; enter thou into the joy of thy Lord."

There are two things in theſe words that particularly deſerve our notice. The *character of thoſe* who ſhall meet with the approbation of their Lord, in the great day of final awards ; they have been *good* and *faithful* ſervants. And the *reward* ſuch ſhall receive, on that ſolemn occaſion, from the judge of quick and dead—They ſhall be each one received with a " Well done, thou good and faithful fervant ; thou haſt been faithful over a few things, I will make thee ruler over many things ; enter thou into the joy of thy Lord."

Agreeably to this view of my text, I ſhall,

I. Briefly conſider the character of the good and faithful fervant of Chriſt.

II. The nature of that reward here promiſed to all ſuch, in the great day of the Lord.

Let us enquire,

I. What is the character of the good and faithful servant of Christ?

I have already said, this may be applied either to the disciples of Christ in general, of whatever nation, denomination, or character in life they may be; or to the Ministers of the Gospel in particular. I shall consider the phrase as including both. And it implies,

1. *Love to Christ and his service.*—A good servant always loves a good master. But it is necessary to observe here, that this love to Christ and his service is not found in the heart of depraved man, in his natural state. We are by nature alienated from God; destitute of every principle of love to him and his son, Christ, in their true character. The apostolic description of depraved human nature is, " having the understanding darkened, being alienated from the life of God, through the ignorance that is in them, because of the blindness of their hearts."* Hence arises the necessity of being " renewed in the spirit of our mind; and of putting on the new man, which after God is created in righteousness and true holiness.† But one of the principal constituents of this new man is, love to God and his son, Christ Jesus. Love to God for his own divine excellence, as well as for the beneficence of his hand, to us—and love to Christ, as being the " brightness of his father's glory, and the express image of his person."‡ The sincere servant of Christ loves both his person and his character. His soul is pleased with him, as he is exhibited in the oracles of truth. " He is the chief among ten thousand, and altogether lovely in his esteem.§ He loves also his *service:* He el-

---

* *Eph. iv.* 18. † *Ver.* 23, 24. ‡ *Heb. i.* 3. § *Song v.* 10, 16.

teems his laws to be altogether equal and just.——
This is the native effect of his love to his person and his government : " For this is the love of
God, that we keep his commandments, and his
commandments are not grievous."* The love we
bear to the person of Christ, in proportion to its
prevalence, will not only induce us to obedience,
but render that obedience easy and delightful——
We delight to oblige those whom we love.

2. The good and faithful servant of Christ *loves
his fellow-servants*—He considers them as children
of the same common father with himself : and we
read, that " every one that loveth him who begat,
loveth him also who is begotten of him."† He
considers them as redeemed by the same precious
blood of Christ ; and as the subjects of the same
sanctifying and comforting influences of the spirit
of grace, which are the common priviledge of
every true Christian ; for " if any man have not
the spirit of Christ, he is none of his."‡ He considers them as engaged in the same common cause
with himself ; the advancement of the kingdom of
Christ, and the illustration of the honour of God
in our world. These are the great ends the good
and faithful servants of Christ have in view, however they may differ in some of the modes of pur-
suing them. Yet this difference does not forfeit
their love, or destroy their charity for each other.
If the person whose character I describe, cannot
agree to agree with his brethren, in denomination,
or mode of worship, he will agree to differ with
them—He will agree they should think and act for
themselves, in matters of such infinite concern ;
a priviledge he justly claims to himself. And in
how many things soever the disciples of Christ may

* 1 John v. 3. † 1 John v. 1. ‡ Rom. viii. 9.

differ in matters of leffer moment, they will all agree in loving their Mafter, his honour, his truth, and his fervice—They will agree in adorning their profeffion in all godlinefs of converfation.

Again—The good and faithful fervant confiders his fellow-difciples as in the fame vale of tears, and in the fame ftate of imperfection and trial with him-felf ; and, therefore, that both they and he ftand in need of mutual fympathy, charity, and forbear-ance, one towards another. In a word, he con-fiders them as heirs of the fame future glory with himfelf ; as " travelling to the fame city, which hath foundations, whofe builder and maker is God ;" and that, therefore, they ought not to dif-fer by the way.

Of fuch importance is this brotherly love, in the Eftimation of our Lord, that he not only enjoins it upon his difciples as their duty, but as their dif-tinguifhing and characteriftic duty ; that duty which more ftrongly marks their character as his difciples than almoft any other ; and that by which they are efpecially to diftinguifh themfelves from the men of the world. You, therefore, hear him fay, " A new commandment I give unto you, that ye love one another ; as I have loved you, that ye alfo love one another. By this fhall all men know that ye are my difciples, if ye have love one to ano-ther."*

3. *Diligence in his Lord's work*, is another in-gredient in the character of the good and faithful fervant. You will eafily perceive the abfurdity of a good, and at the fame time a *flothful* fervant, in common life ; and it is ftill more fo in the cafe be-

* *John xiii* 34, 35.

fore us. We all have our work in life affigned us, in the courfe of a wife Providence : and this is two. fold, our general bufinefs as men and Chriftians, and the fpecial bufinefs of our refpective ftations. Both thefe are fruitful of a variety of duties, too numerous to be recited in this place— They embrace the whole compafs of duty, both moral and pofitive, that we owe to our God, our neighbour, or ourfelves. Nor is there a fingle character we fuftain, or relation we bear, in either of thofe views, but what is the fource of important duties. And if you confider the variety and multiplicity of thefe relations and connexions, you will readily perceive thefe duties muft be numerous, as well as important. But all thefe are fo many claims on the diligence of the fervants of Chrift ; fo many obligations on them to be " not flothful in bufinefs, but fervent in fpirit, ferving the Lord."* We muft be diligent too, that one duty may not interfere with another, for every thing is beautiful its feafon.

Again—Diligence is implied in the idea of *faithfulnefs ;* for the fervant cannot be faithful who is not diligent. No man ever employed a fervant to run idle ; nor can any thing be more contrary to the. defign for which Heaven has made us, than a life of floth and idlenefs, unlefs it be a life of open and undifguifed prophanenefs. The author of our lives has fufficiently marked the great end for which he made us, upon the active powers with which he has endowed us—And this diligence is to be particularly employed in the difcharge of the duties of our feveral ftations in life. This is one way, among others, by which we are to bring forth fruit to the honour of our Lord. " And herein,"

* *Romans xii.* 11.

faith our Saviour, " is my father glorified, that you bear much fruit ; so shall ye be my difciples."*

4. The good and faithful fervant *has a fincere regard to his mafter's honour.* This is the end at which he wifhes and ftudies to aim, in all his actions ; agreeably to the Divine command, " Whether ye eat or drink, or whatfoever ye do, do all to the glory of God."† And in this the fervant of Chrift accords with his mafter ; the great end of whofe incarnation, atonement, and interceffion, on the behalf of finners, was, the illuftration of God's declarative glory. He undertook the vindication of the character and government of God, from the contempt fin had caft upon them ; and in this he fully fucceeded, and appeals to his father, that fo he had done—" I have glorified thee on the earth ; I have finifhed the work which thou gaveth me to do."‡ You will perceive, then, that to aim at the honour of God, as the higheft end of all our actions, is, in a capital inftance, to have the " fame mind in us, which was alfo in Chrift Jefus, our Lord."§ The true fervant of Chrift regards the honour both of his character and of his perfon. By the honour of Chrift's character, I mean his honour as mediator ; particularly as the great atonement for fin, and as our interceffor at his father's right hand. But to honour Chrift under this character, in a proper manner, is not only to profefs our firm faith in thefe doctrines, but to accept him as the Lord our righteoufnefs ; it is to truft in the merit of his atonement, as the fole ground of our acceptance in the fight of God—Thus the good and faithful fervant of Chrift puts the higheft honour in his power upon him, in the character of a Saviour. He practically rifks his very falvation on his ability, fuitablenefs, and willingnefs to fave him.

* *John xv.* 8, † *1 Cor. x.* 31. ‡ *John xvii.* 4. § *Phil. ii.* 5.

I fhall mention but one ingredient more in the character I am at prefent illuftrating, and that is,

5. *Faithfulnefs* in the difcharge of the duties of life. The character under which our text repre-fents the fervants of Chrift, is that of *flewards*, with whom their Lord had entrufted his goods ; to fome he gave more, and to others lefs, to trade withal. But the Apoftle tells us, " That it is required in ftewards, that a man· be found *faithful.*"* And you will pleafe to obferve, our text exprefsly ftiles the true difciple of Chrift, " a good and *faithful* fervant."

This faithfulnefs confifts, principally, in a con-fcientious fincerity and diligence in filling up the duties of our feveral ftations and characters in life. And the great rule by which we are to act, is the will of our Lord and Mafter.

Thus much for the character of the good and faithful fervant.

Let us now proceed to enquire,

II. What is the nature of that reward promifed in our text to all fuch good and faithful fervants ?

And, as it is here defcribed, it implies, princi-pally, the four following things :

1. The *acceptance of their perfons* with God.— This is implied in the character here given them, and reprefented in the parable, as given them by their Lord, when he calls them to give an account

C

* 1 *Cor. iv*, 2.

of their ftewardfhip, *good* and *faithful fervants.*
And you will pleafe farther to obferve, they are
not only acknowledged as good and faithful, but
received with a " Well done, ye good and faithful, fervants." This, indeed, chiefly imports an
approbation of their conduct ; but it is no lefs expreffive of the acceptance of their perfons.

But to eftimate this bleffing in a proper manner, it is neceffary to recollect, that as finners, we
had forfeited all right to this acceptance with
God, and juftly merited his fevere difpleafure. That
we deferve nothing but indignation and wrath, tri-
bulation and anguifh, from him, throughout an
immortality of woe. Yea, that fuch is the nature
of the forfeiture we have made of the Divine favour ; and fuch the juftice of the fentence that
binds us down to fuffer his difpleafure, that, it appears not to have been compatable with the honor
of God, to reverfe the fentence, and reftore the
finner to favour, without an adequate fatisfaction.
And the price paid for this bleffing, the precious
blood of the Son of God, greatly contributes to
enhance its value. But how rich the mercy, for
an heir of Hell to become, in this way, " an heir
of God, and a joint heir with Chrift Jefus !"

e. It implies the *approbation and acceptance of
their fervices for. God,* and his caufe in the world.
Every individual among them fhall be received
with a " Well done,* thou good and faithful fervant, thou haft been faithful over a few things."
Language cannot exprefs the approbation of the
great Judge of quick and dead, in ftronger terms.
But did our time; admit of confidering the many

---

* *The original word Ev, here rendered " well done," has a force
that cannot be fully expreffed in our language.*

imperfections that attend the very beft fervices performed, by the holieft of our Lord's fervants, for him, how deeply ftained they are with guilt, it would ferve, not a little, to illuftrate the riches of that reward conferred upon them, in this acceptance of their fervices for him. And this farther fuggefts, what it is of importance to attend to, that this acceptance of our perfons and fervices, when we come to ftand before unblemifhed purity, is not of merit, but of grace, through the atonement and interceffion of the Divine Mediator. "It is to the praife of the glory of his *grace,* that he makes us accepted in the beloved."* But it is never the lefs certain, for its being of grace.

This acceptance of our perfons and fervices, is of itfelf a high reward, for all we have ever done, or can do, for God, while in this life, were there none other; but this is not all—for,

3. This reward implies *actual and fuperadded honours,* conferred upon the faithful fervants of Chrift, in the great day of God. This is the import of " Thou haft been faithful over a few things, I will make thee ruler over many things." What the nature of thefe honours fhall be, we are not fo clearly taught. Two things, however, feem to be plain refpecting them, in the facred oracles, namely, That they fhall bear fome proportion to our faithfulnefs and diligence in our Lord's fervice here—and, that they fhall be great.

They fhall bear fome proportion to our diligence and faithfulnefs in our Lord's fervice in this life. We read, " There is one glory of the fun, and another glory of the moon, and another glory

* *Ephefians* i. 6.

of the ſtars ; for one ſtar differeth from another in glory—So alſo is the reſurrection of the dead."* Theſe words plainly point us to a difference in the degrees of that glory which ſhall be conferred on the ſeveral ſervants of Chriſt, in the day when he ſhall finiſh the mediatorial ſyſtem, by raiſing the dead, and judging the world in righteouſneſs. They ſhall differ as the ſun differs from the moon, and the moon from the ſtars, and the ſtars one from another. But the ground of this difference will be, the zeal, the diligence, and the faithfulneſs with which his ſervants have ſerved him in this life. I may not ſay their ſucceſs will have no in-fluence on this difference of reward ; for we read, " That they who turn many to righteouſneſs, ſhall ſhine as the ſtars, forever and ever."‡ But when we conſider, that it is an act of mere ſovereignty in God, whether he will ſucceed the faithful la-bours of his ſervants, yea, or not, it is not ſo con-ſonant to our ideas of equity, to make it an equal ground of diſtinguiſhed honours, with thoſe things that are voluntary in us, as our faithfulneſs and diligence, in a great meaſure, are. Beſides, this would be to weaken, if not to deſtroy, the en-couragement to diligence and faithfulneſs, ariſing from thoſe promiſes of reward to them, ſo fre-quent in the oracles of truth ; eſpecially as the moſt diligent and faithful ſervants of Chriſt, are not always the moſt ſucceſsful. And it farther deſerves our notice, that the reward conferred, in our text, on the good ſervant, is founded, not on his *ſucceſs*, but on his *faithfulneſs* : " Thou haſt been *faithful* over a few things, I will make thee ruler over many things."

I ſhall only add, under this particular, that the parable of the ten pounds, entruſted by their Lord

* 1 Cor. xv. 41, 42. ‡ Daniel xii. 3.

to the ten servants, which you have in the nineteenth chapter of the Gospel by Luke, sufficiently demonstrates, that the rewards that shall be conferred on the servants of Christ at last, will not only differ in their degrees of honour, but that this honour shall bear a proportion to their diligence and faithfulness for him in this life. They each one received one pound a piece, as you may perceive by reading the parable. Of these, one, by his diligence and faithfulness, had gained ten pounds, and he is made ruler over ten cities.— Another, by his diligence, had gained five pounds, and he is made ruler over five cities.

You will please to observe, the sums entrusted to these servants were the same ; but the improvement is represented as different, and that the difference in the reward, is proportioned to the difference in the improvement.

The lowest degree, however, of this reward shall be very great to those who receive it. This appears, from the images used in Scripture, to illustrate its nature. It is compared to, it is illustrated by, all the glories of royalty. Hence we read of "a *crown* of righteousness,"* and of "a *crown of glory,* that fadeth not away,"† that shall be conferred upon all the sincere disciples of Christ. Of a *throne,*and their *sitting upon* that throne ; "To him that overcometh, will I grant to sit with me on my throne, even as I also overcame, and am set down with my Father in his throne."‡ We also read of a *kingdom,* and their entering on the possession of that kingdom : " Come ye blessed of my Father, inherit the kingdom prepared for you from the foundation of the world."¶ Agreeably

* 2 *Tim.* iv. 8, † 1 *Pet. v.* 4.‡ *Rev. iii.* 21. ¶ *Matt. xxv.* 34.

to this, the good and faithful fervants of Chrift are faid to be made *kings* and *priefts* unto God.* But a throne, a crown, and a kingdom, are the fummit of earthly grandeur, the utmoft reach of human atchievement. And yet thefe, all thefe, fall infinitely fhort of the bleffednefs and honours, in fure referve for thofe whofe charaƈter I have defcribed : for it is written, " Eye hath not feen, nor ear heard, neither have entered into the heart of man, the things which God hath prepared for them that love him."†

4. The reward in our text includes the *moft con-fummate happinefs, in the immediate prefence and frui-tion of a God in Chrift.* This is imported in that phrafe,"Enter thou into the joy of thy Lord."Thefe are, literally, "Joysunfpeakable,and full of glory." They include all that happinefs that is derived to the fpirits of juft men made perfeƈt, from the cleareft knowledge of a God in Chrift ; from the moft perfeƈt conformity to him, and the fulleft enjoy-ment of him. By the *cleareft* knowledge of a God in Chrift, I do not mean a *perfeƈt* knowledge of him ; for " Who, by fearching, can find out God, or know the Almighty to perfeƈtion ?"‡ But I mean the fulleft knowledge of him, that the then enlarged, and daily enlarging, capacity can poffi-bly receive ; and which, when compared with our prefent knowledge, will be in a fenfe perfeƈt. The clearnefs, precifion, extent, and fatisfaƈtory nature of this knowledge, are expreffed, in Scripture, by " feeing no more darkly through a glafs, but face to face; and knowing,even as alfo we are known."§ And by the ftrong expreffive phrafe of " feeing God's face."¶

*4 *Rev. i.*   † *1 Cor. ii. 9.*   ‡ *Job xi. 7.*   § *1 Cor. xiii. 12.*
¶ *Rev.. xxii.*6 .

This knowledge of God, especially as shining in the face of Christ, is one principal source of that consummate happiness, enjoyed by glorified spirits. They know him as *their* God and portion, and as such their delightful experience recognizes and realizes him. That is an instructive and emphatical phrase, as it lies in the original, Rev. xxi. 3, last clause—which, literally rendered, runs thus, " And God himself shall be with them, their God ;" that is, exhibiting and manifesting himself to them, as their God, in all the ways that their souls, now arrived at the maturity of their existence, both in a natural and moral view, can possibly admit. Every power of the matured mind shall be an avenue, through which blessedness shall flow into it, from God, the fountain of blessedness, throughout an unwasting immortality.

I may not, I dare not undertake to describe the nature of this happiness. I shall only observe respecting it, that our text stiles it " the joy of our Lord"—" Enter thou into the joy of thy Lord"— This, no doubt, means, the joy of our Lord Christ.

It is the joy of our Lord, *because it has been purchased by him.* This reflects a peculiar glory upon it, in the estimation of the spirits of just men made perfect ; it infuses a divine and exquisite relish into it—to this accords their song to him, " Thou art worthy to take the book, and to open the seals thereof ; for thou wast slain, and hast *redeemed us to God by thy blood,* out of every kindred, and tongue, and people, and nation."*

Again—It is the joy of our Lord, *because Christ, our Lord, has taken possession of it in the name of*

* *Rev. v. 9.*

his people—Some of his laſt words to his diſciples were, " I go to prepare a place for you."† He roſe from the dead, and aſcended to glory, not in the character of a private perſon, but as the covenant head and repreſentative of his people—This is the character in which " he has entered into Heaven, as the forerunner for us."‡

It is alſo the joy of our Lord, becauſe it is *derived from God, to the happy ſubjects thereof, through Jeſus Chriſt,* as the *bond of their union with him,* and the *medium of their intercourſe with him*—And this will continue to be the caſe throughout a bleſſed immortality.

And, laſtly, It is the joy of our Lord, becauſe it is a joy *of the ſame kind with that which the glorified human nature of our Lord himſelf ſhares ;* ſo far as they ſhall be capable of it—What leſs than this can be the import of that ſtrong phraſe, " Heirs of God, and *joint heirs* with Chriſt."§ Nor is this all, They ſhall enjoy it in the ſame manſions of bleſſedneſs, which he himſelf inhabits. This is his promiſe to them, " I will come again, and receive you unto myſelf, that *where* I am, there ye may be alſo."§§ And his availing prayer for them is, " Father, I will, that they alſo whom thou haſt given me, *be with me where I am,* that they may behold my glory which thou haſt given me."§§§ Agreeably to which, we read, " They ſhall ever be *with* the Lord."¶

And now from all this, you will not heſitate to conclude, that this joy muſt be a compleat and an everlaſting joy. And, what can it be more ?

† John xiv. 2. ‡ Heb. vi. 20. § Rom. viii. 17. §§ John xiv. 3. §§§ John xvii. 24. ¶ 1 Theſſ. iv. 17.

My brethren, you will eafily perceive this fubject teaches us, the nature of the religion of Jefus
Chrift. It forms its happy fubjects to a proper
temper and a proper conduct towards God and
their neighbours. It makes them good and faithful fervants to their Mafter, who is in Heaven. It
teaches them their duty, and inclines and enables
them to comply with it. Its doctrines and pre-
cepts, its promifes and threatenings, are powerful
principles of action. Thus it is that divine truth
fanctifies the human heart, agreeably to our Lord's
prayer, "Sanctify them through the truth; thy
word is truth."*

You will farther obferve, this religion not only
teaches us our duty, and forms us to it, but rewards us, in the moft glorious manner, for this our
very duty—Rewards us with an immortality of
bleffednefs, in the full enjoyment of the Father of
our Spirits. How grand, interefting, and dignified the fcenes it opens beyond the grave!

Do any of thofe fyftems of morality, which the
fons of infidelity wifh to eftablifh, independent of
the facred Scriptures, furnifh fuch motives to
virtue? Motives fo rational and fo calculated to
influence? It is revelation alone that pufhes its
incentives beyond the grave; that pufhes them
home to the inmoft feelings of the human heart;
that embraces every fpring of action, even the moft
fecret; and touches them in the moft tender, juft,
and energetic manner.

Again—This fubject fuggefts matter of great en-
couragement to the people of God, and efpecially
to the minifters of Chrift, to be faithful and diligent

D

* *John xvii.* 17.

in the work affigned them in life. Our Lord marks, with an omnifcient eye, all our conduct towards him ; and while he reprehends our floth and unfaithfulnefs, he encourages and rewards our meaneft fervices for him. " A cup of cold water given to a difciple, in the name of a difciple," he affures us, " fhall in no wife lofe its reward."* Let us, then, fhake off our floth ; let us up and be doing : Our work is great ; our time is fhort, and our reward glorious. Nor is there a fingle Chriftian, however private his ftation, or obfcure his character, but what may, fome how or other, ferve the interefts of his Lord in the world. This he may do by a confcientious difcharge of the du-ties of the devout, but efpecially of the duties of the focial life. This will exhibit religion in a juft point of light to the furrounding world, and glorify our Father, who is in Heaven.

They may alfo be ufeful in and by the duty of prayer ; fecret and family prayer. Our God is a God who hears prayer ; and he, no doubt, fheds many a blefling on his minifters, on his church, on the commonwealth, and on the world, in anfwer to the prayers of his humble, though obfcure, friends. " Therefore, my beloved brethren, feeing God is not unrighteous to forget your work and labour of love"—" Let us be ftedfaft, unmoveable, always abounding in the work of the Lord, forafmuch as we know our labour is not in vain in the Lord."

But it is time I fhould haften to obferve, that this fubject ftrongly applies to the occafion of my addreffing you this day—The death of that ve-nerable man of God, who prefided, with fo much dignity, over this inftitution for twenty-fix years.

* *Matt. x.* 42.

This great man was defcended from a refpectable parentage ; which had long poffeffed a confiderable landed property in the eaft of Scotland.
His father was minifter of the parifh of Yefter, a
few miles from Edinburgh, where he was born on
the fifth day of February, 1722.* This worthy
man was eminent for his piety, his literature, and
for a habit of extreme accuracy, in all his writings
and difcourfes. This example contributed not a
little to form in his fon that tafte and that love of
accuracy, united with a noble fimplicity, for which
he was fo diftinguifhed through his whole life. He
was fent, very young, to the public fchool at Had-
dington : His father fpared neither expence nor
pains in his education. There he foon acquired
reputation for his affiduity in his ftudies, and for a
native foundnefs of judgment, and clearnefs and
quicknefs of conception, among his fchool-fellows :
many of whom have fince filled the higheft ftations
in the literary and political world.

---

* Dr. Witherfpoon was lineally defcended from that eminent man
of God, the Rev. Mr. John Knox, whom Dr. Robertfon ftiles, " The
prime inftrument of fpreading and eftablifhing the reformed religion
in Scotland." The genius, learning, piety, zeal, and intrepidity of this
great man, rendered him fingularly qualified for the diftinguifhed part he
bore in that interefting event. It is recorded of Mary, Queen of Scots,
that fhe faid, " She was more afraid of John Knox's prayers, than
of an army of ten thoufand men." Worn out by inceffant labours,
he died on the 27th day of November, 1572, in the 67th year of his
age. The Earl of Morton, then Regent of Scotland, who attended
his funeral, pronounced his eulogium in a few words ; the more honourable for Mr. Knox, fays the above hiftorian, as they came from
one whom he had often cenfured, with peculiar feverity, " Here lies
he who never feared the face of man." Mr. Knox's daughter Eliza-
beth married the famous Mr. John Welfh, who ftrongly refembled his
father-in-law in genius, character, and ufefulnefs in the church :
And in this line Dr. Witherfpoon defcended from this honourable an-
ceftry.

At the age of fourteen, he was removed to the univerfity of Edinburgh. Here he continued, attending the different profeffors, with a high degree of credit, in all the branches of learning, until the age of twenty-one, when he was licenfed to preach the Gofpel. In the theological hall, particularly, he was remarked for a moft judicious tafte in facred criticifm, and for a precifion of idea and perfpicuity of expreffion rarely attained at that early period.

Immediately on his leaving the univerfity, he was invited to be affiftant minifter with his father, with the right of fucceffion to the charge. But he chofe rather to accept an invitation from the parifh of Beith, in the weft of Scotland. Here he was ordained to the work of the gofpel miniftry, and fettled with the univerfal acquiefcence, and even with the fervent attachment of the people : A circumftance which, under the patronage that unhappily exifts in that church, is but too rarely the cafe in the fettlement of their clergy. His character as a preacher, which rendered him fo acceptable and popular, will come more naturally before us in another place. Let it fuffice to remark here, that, always interefting and inftructive in the pulpit, he was affiduous in the difcharge of every parochial duty when out of it. And his preaching generally turned on thofe great, diftinguifhing, and practical truths of the gofpel, which, in every Chriftian country, moft affect and attach the hearts of the great body of the people.

From Beith he was, after a few years, tranflated to the large and flourifhing town of Paifly, fo celebrated for its various and fine manufactures.— Here he refided in the height of reputation and ufefulnefs; and riveted in the affections of his people, and his fellow-citizens, when he was called to the presidency of this college.

During his residence at Paisly, he was invited to Dublin, in Ireland, to assume the charge of a numerous and respectable congregation in that city. He was also called to Rotterdam, in the Republic of the United Provinces—and to the town of Dundee, in his own country. But he could not be induced to quit a sphere of such respectability, comfort, and usefulness. He rejected also, in the first instance, the invitation of the trustees of this college. He thought it almost impossible for him to break connexions at home, that had been so long endeared to him—to violate all the attachments and habits of the female part of his family—to leave the scene of his happiness and honour—and, in his middle career, to bury himself, as he apprehended, in a new and distant country.

But warmly urged by all those friends whose judgment he most respected, and whose friendship he most esteemed—and hoping that he might repay his sacrifices, by greater usefulness to the cause of the Redeemer, and to the interests of learning, in this new world—and knowing that this institution had been consecrated, from its foundation, to those great objects to which he had devoted his life, he finally consented, on a second application, to wave every other consideration, to cross the ocean, and to take among us that important charge to which he had been called, with the concurrent wishes, and the highest expectations, of all the friends of the college.* Their expectations have not been

* *Dr. Witherspoon arrived with his family at Princeton in the month of August, 1768. He was the sixth President of the College since its foundation in the year 1746. His predecessors were, the Rev. Messrs.* Jonathan Dickenson, Aaron Burr, Jonathan Edwards,

difappointed. Its reputation and fuccefs, under his adminiftration, have been equal to our moft fanguine hopes.

Almoft the firft benefit which it received, befides the eclat, and the aeceffion of ftudents, procured to it by the fame of his literary charaƈer, was the augmentation of its funds. The college has never enjoyed any refources from the ftate. It was founded, and has been fupported, wholly by private liberality and zeal. And its finances, from a variety of caufes, were in a low and declining condition, at the period when Dr. Witherfpoon arrived in America. But his reputation excited an uncommon liberality in the public ; and his perfonal exertions, extended from Maffachufetts to Virginia, foon raifed its funds to a flourifhing ftate. The war of the revolution, indeed, afterwards, proftrated every thing, and almoft annihilated its refources ; yet we cannot but with gratitude recolleƈt, how much the inftitution owed, at that time, to his enterprize and his talents.

But the principal advantages it derived, were from his literature ; his fuperintendancy ; his example as a happy model of good writing ; and from the tone and tafte which he gave to the literary purfuits of the college.

In giving the outlines of the charaƈter of this great man, for I attempt no more, I fhall begin

Samuel Davies, *and Dr.* Samuel Finley—*Men defervedly celebrated for genius, learning, and piety. Mr. Dickinfon and Mr. Edwards were advanced in life when chofen to the prefidency.*

Not long before Dr. Witherfpoon left Scotland, and while in fufpence refpeƈling his duty, a gentleman, poffeffed of a confiderable property, an old bachelor, and a relation of the family, promifed to make him his heir, if he would not go to America.

with obferving, that perhaps his principal merit appeared in the pulpit. He was, in many ref_pects, one of the beft models on which a young preacher could form himfelf. It was a fingular felicity to the whole college, but efpecially to thofe who had the profeffion of the miniftry in view, to have fuch an example conftantly before them. Religion, by the manner in which it was treated by him, always commanded the refpect of thofe who heard him, even when it was not able to engage their hearts. An admirable textuary, a profound theologian, perfpicuous and fimple in his manner; an univerfal fcholar, acquainted deeply with human nature; a grave, dignified, and folemn fpeaker, he brought all the advantages derived from thefe fources to the illuftration and enforce-ment of divine truth. Though not a fervent and animated orator,* he was always a folemn, affect-ing, and inftructive preacher. It was impoffible to hear him without attention, or to attend to him without improvement. He had a happy talent at unfolding the ftrict and proper meaning of the fa-cred writer, in any text from which he chofe to difcourfe; at concentrating and giving perfect unity to every fubject which he treated; and pre-

---

* *A peculiar affection of his nerves, which always overcame him when he allowed himfelf to feel very fervently on any fubject, obliged him, from his earlieft entrance on public life, to impofe a ftrict ref-traint and guard upon his fenfibility. He was, therefore, under the neceffity of fubftituting gravity and ferioufnefs of manner, in public fpeaking, in the room of that fire and warmth, of which he was well capable, by nature; and which he fo much admired in others, when managed with prudence.*

He never read his fermons, or ufed fo much as fhort notes, in the pulpit. His practice was, to write his fermons at full length, and commit them to memory; but not confine himfelf to the precife words he had penned. He often took great liberties, in the delivery of his difcourfes, to alter, add to, or abridge what he had written; but this never infringed upon the ftricteft accuracy.

senting to the hearer the moſt clear and compre-
henſive views of it. His ſermons were diſtinguiſhed
for their judicious and perſpicuous diviſions—for
mingling profound remarks on human life, along
with the illuſtration of divine truth—and for the
lucid order that reigned through the whole. In
his diſcourſes, he loved to dwell chiefly on the
great doﬁrines of divine grace, and on the diſtin-
guiſhing truths of the goſpel. Theſe he brought,
as far as poffible, to the level of every under-
ſtanding, and the feeling of every heart. He ſel-
dom choſe to lead his hearers into ſpeculative dif-
cuffions, and never to entertain them by a mere
diſplay of talents. All oſtentation in the pulpit,
he viewed with the utmoſt averſion and contempt.
During the whole of his preſidency, he was ex-
tremely ſolicitous to train thoſe ſtudious youths,
who had the miniſtry of the goſpel in view, in ſuch
a manner, as to ſecure the greateſt reſpeﬁability,
as well as uſefulneſs, in that holy profeffion. It
was his conſtant advice to young preachers, never
to enter the pulpit without the moſt careful preparation. It was his ambition and his hope, to
render the ſacred miniſtry the moſt learned, as well
as the moſt pious and exemplary body of men in
the Republic.

As a writer, his ſtile is ſimple and comprehen-
ſive—his remarks judicious, and often refined—
his information, on every ſubjeﬁ which he
treats, accurate and extenſive—his matter always
weighty and important—cloſely condenſed, and yet
well arranged and clear. Simplicity, perſpicuity,
preciſion, comprehenſion of thought, and knowledge of the world, and of the human heart, reign
in every part of his writings. Three volumes of
eſſays, and two volumes of ſermons, beſides ſeveral
detached diſcourſes, already publiſhed—and treat-

ing chiefly on the moſt important and practical
ſubjects in religion—have deſervedly extended his
reputation, not only through Britain, Ireland, and
America, but through moſt of the proteſtant coun-
tries of Europe. His remarks on the nature and
effects of the ſtage, enter deeply into the human
heart. We find there many refined obſervations,
after the example of the Meſſieurs de Port-Royal
in France, not obvious to ordinary minds, but
perfectly founded in the hiſtory of man, and the
ſtate of ſociety. The pernicious influence of that
amuſement on the public taſte and morals, was, perhaps, never more clearly elucidated. On the following intereſting ſubjects, the *nature and neceſſity of re-
generation— Juſtification by free grace, through Jeſus
Chriſt;* and *the importance of truth in religion,* or, the
*connexion that ſubſiſts between found principles and a
holy practice,* there is, perhaps, nothing ſuperior in
the Engliſh language. But Dr. Witherſpoon's talents were various. He was not only a ſerious
writer, but he poſſeſſed a fund of refined humour,
and delicate ſatire. A happy ſpecimen of this is
ſeen in his *Eccleſiaſtical Characteriſtics.* The edge
of his wit, in that performance, was directed againſt
certain corruptions in principle and practice pre-
valent in the church of Scotland. And no attack
that was ever made upon them, gave them ſo deep
a wound, or was ſo ſeverely felt. Dr. Warburton,
the celebrated Biſhop of Glouceſter, mentions the
Characteriſtics with particular approbation, and
expreſſes his wiſh, that the Engliſh church, as ſhe
needed too, had likewiſe ſuch a corrector.

This may be the proper place to mention his
general character, as a member of the councils and
courts of the church, and the part particularly that
he took in the eccleſiaſtical politics of his native

country. The church of Scotland was divided into two parties, with refpect to their ideas of ecclefiaftical difcipline. The one was willing to con-
firm, and even extend the rights of *patronage*—the
other wifhed, if poffible, to abrogate, or at leaft
limit them, and to extend the rights and influence
of the people, in the fettlement and removal of
minifters. The latter were zealous for the doctrines of grace, and the articles of religion, in all
their ftrictnefs, as contained in their national con-
feffion of faith. The former were willing to allow
a greater latitude of opinion ; and they preached
in a ftile that feemed to the people lefs evangelical,
and lefs affecting to the heart and confcience, than
that of their opponents. In their concern, like-
wife, to exempt the clergy of their party from the
unreafonable effects of popular caprice, they too
frequently protected them againft the juft com-
plaints of the people. Thefe were ftiled *moderate
men*, while their antagonifts were diftinguifhed by
the name of the *orthodox*. Dr. Witherfpoon, in
his church politics, early and warmly embraced
the fide of the orthodox. This he did from con-
viction, and a fenfe of duty ; and, by degrees,
acquired fuch an influence in their councils, that
he was confidered at length as their head and leader. Before he had acquired this influence, their
councils were managed without union and addrefs,
while the meafures of the moderate party had, for
a long time, been conducted by fome of the greateft
literary characters in the nation. It had happened
among the orthodox, as it often does among fcru-
pulous and confcientious men, who are not verfed
in the affairs of the world, that each purfued inflex-
ibly his own opinion, as the dictate of an honeft
confcience. He could not be induced to make any
modification of it, in order to accommodate it to
the views of others. He thought that all addrefs

and policy, was ufing too much management with confcience. Hence refulted difunion of meafures, and confequent defeat—But Dr. Witherfpoon's enlarged mind did not refufe to combine *the wifdom of the ferpent with the harmleffnefs of the dove.* He had, probably, the principal merit of creating among them union, and harmony of defign; of concentrating their views, and giving fyftem to their operations. One day, after carrying fome important queftions in the general affembly, againft the celebrated Dr. Robertfon, who was at that time confidered as the leader of the oppofite party, the latter faid to him, in a pleafant and eafy manner, " I think you have your men better difciplined than formerly." "Yes (replied Dr. Witherfpoon) by urging your politics too far, you have compelled us to beat you with your own weapons."

We have feen him in our own church judicatories, in America, always upright in his views—remarkable for his punctuality in attending upon them—and able to feize, at once, the right point of view on every queftion—able to difentangle the moft embaraffed fubjects—clear and conclufive in his reafonings—and from habit in bufinefs, as well as from a peculiar foundnefs of judgment, always conducting every difcuffion to the moft fpeedy and decifive termination. The church has certainly loft in him, one of her greateft lights; and, if I may ufe the term in ecclefiaftical affairs, one of her greateft *politicians.*

Before entering on his talents as a prefident, fuffer me, in a fentence or two, to call to your mind his focial qualities. When not engaged in the great and ferious bufineffes of life, he was one of the moft companionable of men. Furnifhed with a rich fund of anecdote, both amufing and inftructive; his moments of relaxation were as entertaining, as his ferious ones were fraught with improvement. One quality remarkable, and highly deferving imitation in him was, *his attention to young perfons.* He never fuffered an opportunity to efcape him of imparting the moft ufeful advice to them, according to their circumftances, when they happened to be in his company. And this was always done in fo agreeable a way, that they could neither be inattentive to it, nor was it poffible to forget it.

On his domeftic virtues I fhall only fay, he was an affectionate hufband, a tender parent, and a kind mafter; to which I may add, he was a fincere and a warm friend.—But, I haften to confider him as a fcholar, and a director of the fyftem of education in the college.

An univerfal fcholar himfelf, he endeavoured to eftablifh the fyftem of education in this inftitution, upon the moft extenfive and refpectable bafis, that its fituation and its finances would admit. Formerly, the courfe of inftruction had been too fuperficial; and its metaphyfics and philofophy were too much tinctured with the dry and uninftructive forms of the fchools. This, however, was by no means to be imputed as a defect, to thofe great and excellent men, who had prefided over the inftitution before him; but rather to the recent origin of the country—the imperfection of its ftate of fociety—and to the ftate of literature in it. Since his prefidency mathematical fcience has received an extenfion, that was not known before in the American feminaries. He introduced into philofophy, all the moft liberal and modern improvements of Europe. He extended the philofophical courfe to embrace the general principles of policy and public law ; he incorporated with it a found and rational metaphyfics—equally remote from the doctrines of fatality and contingency—from the barrennefs and dogmatifm of the fchools—and from the exceffive refinements of thofe contradictory, but equally impious fects of fcepticifm, who wholly deny the exiftence of matter, or maintain that nothing but matter exifts in the univerfe.

He laid the foundation of a courfe of hiftory in the college—and the principles of tafte, and the rules of good writing, were both happily explained by him, and exemplified in his *manner.* The *flile* of *learning,* if you will allow me the phrafe, has been changed by him. Literary inquiries and improvements have become more liberal, more extenfive, and more profound. An admirable faculty for governing, and of exciting the emulation of the young gentlemen under his care, contributed to give fuccefs to all his defigns, for perfecting the courfe of inftruction. The numbers of men of diftinguifhed talents, in the different liberal profeffions, in this country, who have received the elements of their education under him, teftify his fervices to the college. Under his aufpices have been formed a large proportion of the clergy of our church ; and to his inftructions, America owes many of her moft diftinguifhed patriots and legiflators*.

Thus he proceeded, guiding with uncommon reputation and fuccefs the courfe of education in this inftitution, until the war of the American revolution fufpended his functions and difperfed the college.

* *More than thirty members of the congrefs of United America, fince the formation of that illuftrious body, have been fons of the college of New-Jerfey ; and amongft thefe, fome of their firft characters for reputation and ufefulnefs.*

Here he entered upon a new scene, and appeared in a new character; widely differing from any, in which he had been heretofore presented to the public. Yet, here also, he shone with equal lustre; and his talents as a legislator and senator shewed the extent and the variety of the powers of his mind. There are few foreigners who can, with such facility as he did, lay aside their prejudices, and enter into the ideas and habits of a new country, and a new state of society. He became almost at once an American, on his landing among us, and in the unjust war which Great-Britain waged against us, he immediately adopted the views, and participated in the councils of the Americans. His distinguished abilities soon pointed him out to the citizens of New-Jersey, as one of the most proper delegates to that convention which formed their republican constitution. In this respectable assembly he appeared, to the astonishment of all the professors of the law, as profound a *civilian*, as he had before been known to be a *philosopher* and *divine*.

From the revolutionary committees and conventions of the state, he was sent, early in the year 1776, as a representative of the people of New-Jersey to the congress of United America; he was seven years a member of that illustrious body, which, under providence, in the face of innumerable difficulties and dangers, led us on to the establishment of our independence. Always firm in the most gloomy and formidable aspects of public affairs, and always discovering the greatest reach and presence of mind, in the most embarrassing situations.

It is impossible here to enter into all his political ideas. It is but justice however to observe, that on almost all subjects on which he differed from the majority of his brethren in congress, his principles have been justified by the result. I shall select only one or two examples. He constantly opposed the expensive mode of supplying the army *by commission*, which was originally adopted; and combated it, until after a long experience of its ill effects, he, in conjunction with a few firm and judicious associates, prevailed to have it done by contract.*

He opposed, at every emission after the first or second, and even hazarded his popularity for a time by the strenuousness of his opposition, that paper currency which gave such a wound to public credit, and which would have defeated the revolution, if any thing could.†

In the formation of the original confederation, he complained of the jealousy and ambition of the individual states, which were not willing to entrust the general government, with adequate powers for the common interest. He then pronounced inefficacy upon it. But he complained and remonstrated in vain.‡

---

* *Congress at first supplied the army by allowing a certain commission per cent. on the monies that the commissioners expended. This invited expence. At length they were induced to agree to the mode by contract; or allowing to the purchaser a certain sum per ration.*

† *Instead of emissions of an unfounded paper, beyond a certain quantum, Dr. Witherspoon urged the propriety of making loans, and establishing funds for the payment of the interest; which in the temper of the public mind, he thought could then have been easily effected. America has since regretted that she had not pursued that policy. The doctor afterwards, at the instance of some of the very gentlemen who opposed him in congress, published his ideas on the nature, value and uses of money, in one of the most clear and judicious essays that, perhaps, was ever written on the subject.*

‡ *He particularly remonstrated against the tardy, inefficient and faithless manner of providing for the public exigencies and debts, by*

Overruled however, at that time, in these and
in other objects of importance, he had the satisfac-
tion of living to see America revert, in almost every
instance, to his original ideas—Ideas founded on a
sound and penetrating judgment, and matured by
deep reflection, and an extensive observation of
men and things. But I forbear to trace his political career farther; and shall only add here, that
while he was thus engaged in serving his country in
the character of a *civilian*, he did NOT lay aside
his *ministry*. He gladly embraced every opportunity of preaching, and of discharging the other duties of his office, as a gospel minister. This he
considered as his highest character, and honor in
life.

The college having been collected as soon as
possible after its dispersion, instruction was recom-
menced under the immediate care of the vice-pre-
sident.* Dr. Witherspoon's name, however, con-

requisition on the several states. *He insisted on the propriety and necessity, of the government of the union holding in its own hands the
entire regulation of commerce, and the revenues that might be derived
from that source. These he contended would be adequate to all the
wants of the United States, in a season of peace.*

* *The reverend Dr. Samuel S. Smith, who was unanimously chosen
Dr. Witherspoon's successor, on the sixth day of May, 1795. This
gentleman's character needs no eulogium in this place. His several
publications, and particularly his ingenious essay on " The causes of
the variety of complexion and figure of the human species," delivered
before the Philosophical Society, in Philadelphia, February 28th
1787, afford sufficient testimony of his genius and learning. The last
mentioned work has distinguished him in the estimation of the literati,
both in Europe and America. As soon as it made its appearance in
Europe, it was read with avidity—it shortly passed under more edi-
tions than one in Great-Britain—it was translated into the French
language, and published, with great eclat, at Paris—and has been
since translated into the German language, and published with anno-
tations, by a professor of moral philosophy, in one of the universities of
that empire.*

tinued to add celebrity to the inftitution; and it has fully recovered its former reputation.

The glorious ftruggle for our liberties drawing to an honourable period, and the doctor feeling age advancing upon him, was defirous of refigning his place in congrefs : and would have fain retired, in a meafure, from the burdens of the college.

But notwithftanding his wifh for repofe, he was induced, through his attachment to the inftitution, over which he had fo long prefided, once more to crofs the ocean to promote its benefit. The fruit of that voyage was not indeed anfwerable to our wifhes ; but we are not the lefs indebted to his en-terprize and zeal.

After his return to this country, finding nothing to obftruct his entering on that retirement, which was now become more dear to him ; he withdrew, in a great meafure, except on fome important occa-fions, from the exercife of thofe public funtions that were not immediately connected with the du-ties of his office, as prefident of the college, or his character as a minifter of the gofpel.

Accuftomed to order and regularity in bufinefs from his youth, he perfevered in his attention to them through his whole life. And I may add, there was nothing in which his punctuality and exactnefs were more facredly obferved, than in the devotional exercifes of the chriftian life. Befides the daily devotions of the clofet, and the family, it was his ftated practice to obferve the laft day of every year, with his family, as a day of fafting, humilia-tion and prayer : and it was alfo his practice, to fet apart days for fecret fafting and prayer, as occafion fuggefted.

F

Bodily infirmities began at length to come upon him. For more than two years before his death, he was afflicted with the lofs of fight; which contributed to haften the progrefs of his other diforders. Thefe he bore with a patience, and even a cheerfulnefs, rarely to be met with, in the moft eminent for wifdom and piety. Nor would his active mind, and his defire of ufefulnefs to the end, permit him, even in this fituation, to defift from the exercife of his miniftry, and his duties in the college, as far as his health and ftrength would admit. He was frequently led into the pulpit, both at home and abroad, during his blindnefs; and always acquitted himfelf with his ufual accuracy, and frequently, with more than his ufual folemnity and animation. And we all recollect the propriety and dignity with which he prefided at the laft commencement. He was bleft with the ufe of his reafoning powers to the very laft.

At length, however, he funk under the accumulated preffure of his infirmities; and on the 15th day of November, 1794, in the feventy third year of his age, he retired to his eternal reft, full of honor and full of days—there to receive the plaudit of his Lord, " well done thou good and faithful fervant, thou haft been faithful over a few things, be thou ruler over many things; enter thou into the joy of thy Lord."

F I N I S.